This edition 2003

Franklin Watts
96 Leonard Street
London
EC2A 4XD

Franklin Watts Australia
45-51 Huntley Street
Alexandria
NSW 2015

Design: Edward Kinsey
Typesetting: Tradespools Ltd

A CIP catalogue record for this book is available from the British Library.

ISBN: 0 7496 5043 5

Printed in Italy

The publisher would like to thank the Goldman family
and all other people shown in this book.

Due to certain requirements of Jewish Law, some situations shown here
were specifically created for this book.

Note: Many of the photographs in this book
originally appeared in 'My Belief: I am a Jew'

Jewish

Jenny Wood

Photographs: Chris Fairclough
Consultant: Clive Lawton

W

FRANKLIN WATTS
LONDON•SYDNEY

These people are Jews.
They follow the Jewish religion.
Family life is very important
in the Jewish religion.

Every week, Jews celebrate Shabbat.
This is a day of joy and rest.
It starts at sunset every Friday.
The mother lights candles
and gives thanks to God.

The father gives the children
a blessing from the Bible.

The best plates and glasses
are used for the Shabbat meals.
Supper starts with a glass of wine
to celebrate this special day.

When Shabbat ends, a special candle
is lit, and a cup of wine is filled
to overflowing. This is a sign
that the joy of Shabbat should
"spill over" to the new week.

Jewish people have rules
about what they eat.
When food fits these rules,
it is called "kosher".

Meat must be kept separate
from milk or dairy products.
Kosher kitchens have two sets
of plates, pots and cutlery –
one for meat, one for milk foods.

Jews go to pray in a synagogue.
Families meet there,
and hold services.
Most synagogues have
a Jewish teacher called a rabbi.

The Bible scrolls are kept
in the synagogue, in a cupboard
called the Ark. During a service,
the big scroll is carried round
and part of it is read out.

Rabbi's seat

Ark behind the curtain

Women's section

Platform from which services are led

Men and women sit separately
in most synagogues. Services are led
from a platform in the middle.
Any man in the synagogue
can lead a service.

The synagogue also has classrooms
where Jewish children learn
about Jewish laws and customs. They
sing songs and read Bible stories.

In spring, Jews celebrate Passover.
All the members of a family eat
a special meal. They hold a service
in the home, with questions,
stories, games and songs.

At the Passover meal,
all sorts of foods
are placed on a special plate
in the middle of the table.

For Sukkot, the harvest festival,
a special shelter is made
and decorated with leaves,
branches, fruit and pictures.

Sukkot lasts for a week.
During that time, all meals
are eaten in the shelter.

Hanukka is a winter festival.
It lasts for eight days.
On each night, a candle is lit.

Hanukka is a time for playing games
and giving presents
to friends and family.

Purim is a festival
which comes at the end of winter.
There are fancy dress parties
to go to and plays to put on.

The synagogue has a carnival feeling at Purim. Presents are given, especially to people who are too old or ill to leave their homes.

Jewish people try to remember God
in everything they do.
Giving presents reminds them
to look after other people.

FACTS ABOUT JEWS

The Jews are an ancient people with a history stretching back 3,500 years.

Jews believe in one God. They try to live according to the teachings laid down in the Jewish Bible.

The Jewish Bible is what Christians call the Old Testament.

Jewish law forbids the eating of certain foods including pork and shellfish.

To show respect to God, Jewish men cover their heads when praying. Many of them wear a little hat called a kipa.

The scrolls on which the Jewish Holy Book is written are handwritten by people called scribes. It takes a scribe about a year to write a scroll.

There are about 14 million Jews in the world. About a quarter live in Israel, and over a third live in America.

GLOSSARY

Purim
The Jewish "carnival" festival at the end of winter.

Rabbi
A Jewish teacher.

Shabbat
The Jewish day of rest and celebration. It lasts from sunset on Friday to Saturday evening.

Sukkot
The Jewish harvest festival.

Synagogue
The Jewish place of worship.

Ark
A cupboard in the synagogue where the scrolls of the Jewish Holy Book are kept.

Hanukka
The Jewish winter festival of light.

Kosher
Anything that fits Jewish laws. It is mostly used about food, but can be used to describe anything else.

Passover
The Jewish spring festival of freedom.

INDEX

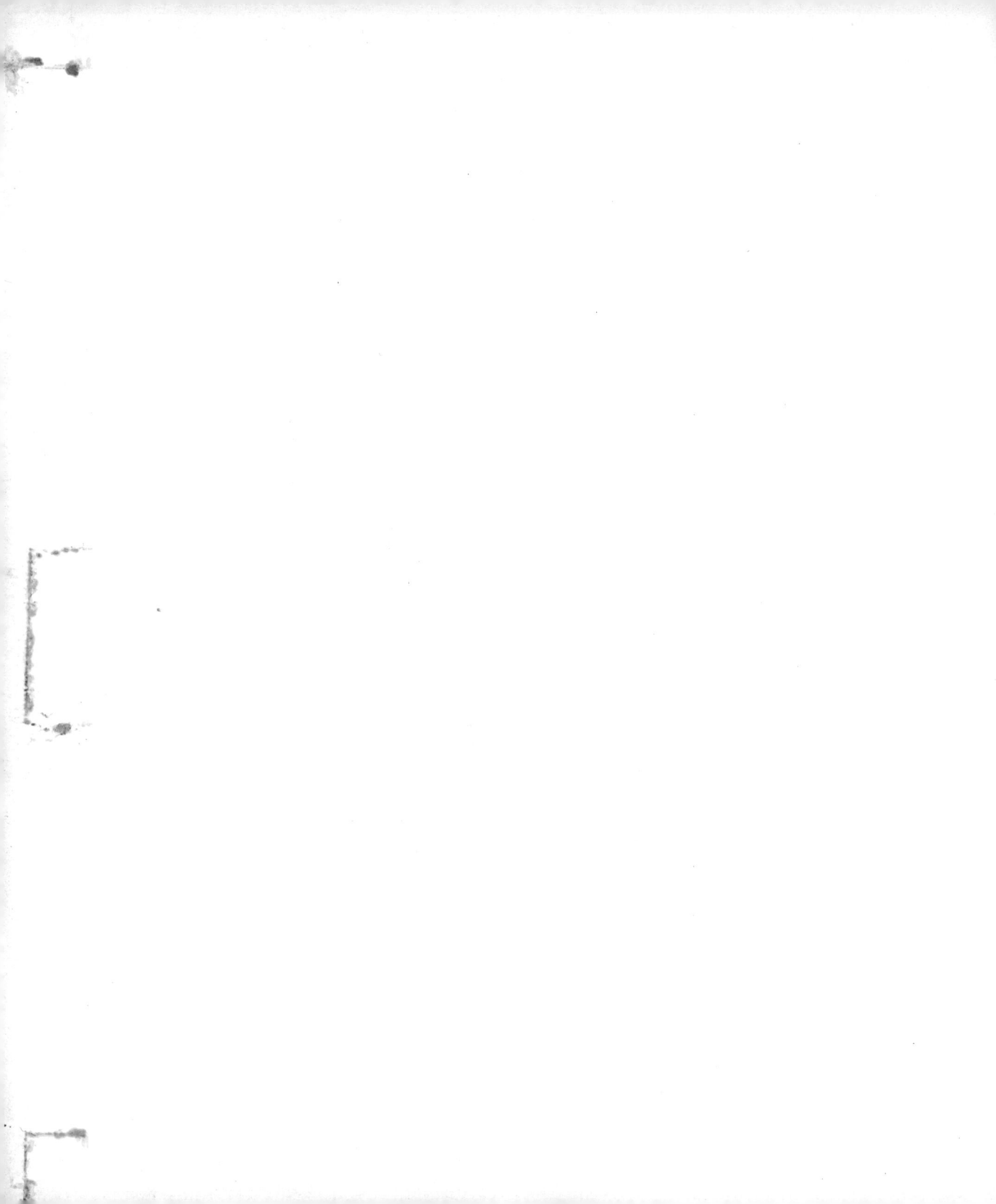